The Nearness of You

The Nearness of You

Carolyn Kizer

POEMS BY CAROLYN KIZER

Copper Canyon Press : Port Townsend 1986

The publication of this book was made possible by a grant from the National Endowment for the Arts.

Copper Canyon Press is in residence with Centrum at Fort Worden State Park.

ISBN: 0-914742-96-5 (cloth)
ISBN: 0-914742-97-3 (paper)
Library of Congress Catalog Card Number: 86-71838

The typefaces are Aldus and Palatino
Cover art is a monotype by Jim Johnson

COPPER CANYON PRESS
Post Office Box 271
Port Townsend, WA 98368

ACKNOWLEDGMENTS

Many of these poems appeared in *The Ungrateful Garden, Knock Upon Silence,* and *Midnight Was My Cry,* all of which have been out of print for a number of years.

"Promising Author" appeared in *The Berkeley Review.*
"The Glass," "The Light," and "The Gift" were printed in *Calapooya 8.*
"Heart's Limbo" appeared in *Poetry,* but has since been revised.
"My Good Father" was printed in *Shenandoah* with the title, "Notes for a Study Club Paper." "Horseback" was also printed in *Shenandoah.*
"To an Unknown Poet" and "Final Meeting" were printed by *The Michigan Quarterly Review.*
"Dangerous Games," "Antique Father," "Afternoon Happiness," and "Reading Your Poems in Your House while You Are Away" are from my book, *Yin.* "Thrall" is from my book, *Mermaids in the Basement.*

"The Nearness of You" is the title of a song by Ned Washington and Hoagy Carmichael (©1937 and 1940 by Famous Music Corporation).

I wish to thank my dear friends, John Montague and Kenneth O. Hanson, for their meticulous reading of this book in manuscript and for their suggestions. Thanks are also due to my equally meticulous and devoted editor, Tree Swenson.

TABLE OF CONTENTS

III. Father

IV. Friends

For the men I love,
especially John

Afternoon Happiness

At a party I spy a handsome psychiatrist,
And wish, as we all do, to get her advice for free.
Doctor, I'll say, I'm supposed to be a poet.
All life's awfulness has been grist to me.
We learn that happiness is a Chinese meal,
While sorrow is a nourishment forever.
My new environment is California Dreamer.
I'm fearful I'm forgetting how to brood.
And, Doctor, another thing has got me worried:
I'm not drinking as much as I should....

At home, I want to write a happy poem
On love, or a love poem of happiness.
But they won't do, the tensions of everyday,
The rub, the minor abrasions of any two
Who share one space. Ah, there's no substitute for tragedy!
But in this chapter, tragedy belongs
To that other life, the old life before *us*.
Here is my aphorism of the day:
Happy people are monogamous,
Even in California. So how does the poem play

Without the paraphernalia of betrayal and loss?
I don't have a jealous eye or fear
And neither do you. In truth, I'm fond
Of your ex-mate, whom I name, "my wife-in-law."
My former husband, that old disaster, is now just funny,
So laugh we do, in what Cyril Connolly
Has called the endless, nocturnal conversation
Of marriage. Which may be the best part.
Darling, must I love you in light verse
Without the tribute of profoundest art?

Of course it won't last. You will break my heart
Or I yours, by dying. I could weep over that.
But now it seems forced, here in these heaven hills,
The mourning doves mourning, the squirrels mating,
My old cat warm in my lap, here on our terrace
As from below comes a musical cursing
As you mend my favorite plate. Later of course
I could pick a fight; there is always material in that.
But we don't come from fighting people, those
Who scream out red-hot iambs in their hate.

No, love, the heavy poem will have to come
From *temps perdu*, fertile with pain, or perhaps
Detonated by terrors far beyond this place
Where the world rends itself, and its tainted waters
Rise in the east to erode our safety here.
Much as I want to gather a lifetime thrift
And craft, my cunning skills tied in a knot for you,
There is only this useless happiness as gift.

I.

MANHOOD

By the Riverside

Do not call from memory — all numbers have changed.

FROM THE COVER OF THE
TELEPHONE DIRECTORY

Once I lived at a Riverside
1-3-7-5, by a real stream, Hangman's Creek,
Named from an old pine, down the hill
On which three Indians died. As a child,
I modeled the Crucifixion on that tree
Because I'd heard two Indians were thieves
Strung up by soldiers from Fort Wright in early days,
But no one remembered who the third one was.

Once, in winter, I saw an old Indian wade,
Breaking the thin ice with his thighs.
His squaw crouched modestly in the water,
But he stood up tall, buck-naked. "Cold!" he said,
Proud of his iron flesh, the color of rust.
He grinned as he spoke, struck his hard chest a blow
Once, with his fist. . . . So I call, from memory,
That tall old Indian, standing in the water.

And I am not put off by an operator
Saying, "Sor-ree, the lion is busy. . . ."
Then, I would tremble, seeing a real lion
Trammeled in endless, golden coils of wire,
Pawing a switchboard in some mysterious
Central office, where animals ran the world,
As I knew they did. To the brave belonged the power.
Christ was a brave, beneath that gauzy clout.

I whispered to the corners of my room, where lions
Crowded at night, blotting the walls with shadows,

As the wind tore at a gutter beneath the eaves,
Moaned with the power of quiet animals
And the old pine, down the hill,
                              where Indians hung:
Telling my prayers, not on a pale-faced Sunday
Nor to a red God, who could walk on water
When winter hardened, and the ice grew stronger.

Now I call up god-head and manhood, both,
As they emerged for a child by the Riverside.
But they are all dead Indians now. They answer
Only to me. The numbers have not changed.

What Was in a Name

Thomas Love Peacock! Thomas Love Peacock!
I used to croon, sitting on the pot,
My sympathetic magic, at age three.
These elements in balance captured me:
Love in the middle, on his right hand a saint
And doubter. Gentle a Kempis, Thomas the Rhymer,
Wyatt, Campion, Traherne, came later.

On Love's left hand, the coarse essentials:
Skimp them, and Love, denying, slides away
Into pure Thomas, etiolated sainthood.
Before cock, the satisfying sound of liquid
Which, as it strikes against the enamel basin,
Proclaims a bodily creativity.
Then Love springs eternal; then cock comes

Demonstrating Love. The surname is complete:
Its barbed crest, its thousand eyes, its harsh cries.
Thomas Love Peacock! Thomas Love Peacock!
The person unsung, the person ritually sung.
But that was thirty years ago; a child's loving
Of God the body, flesh of poetry.
I hail the three-in-one, the one-in-three.

To A Visiting Poet in a College Dormitory

Here tame boys fly down the long light of halls
In this late nightmare of your fourth decade:
Medley of shoe-thuds, towel-slaps and horseplay,
Murmurous radios, counterpoint of squalling
Bed-springs and shower-pipes across your ceiling.

Nocturnal soundings turn you back always
To a broken fountain, faces damp as leaves
Stuck to the fountain's lip in autumn, draining
From an era swamped in war's impersonal seas.
Do you sleep empty and long, or cannonading

Through these nautical chambers, having gathered all
Your strength into one battered bowling ball,
Asleep, ramp up and down these corridors of boys
Barely knocking at doors, but bursting into
Identical rooms, like icicles ablaze?

Now, as I hope you sleep, I turn the pages
Of your committed life — rather the notations
Of sensation coaxed and cheated into poems:
Loves are interred three deep, or rise like drowned
Ruined choristers, to flaunt your praises.

Fisher of bodies, when the lure is failing,
Still you proffer the old nibble of boy-bait,
Though nothing comes now, arias or kingdoms;
You may not deny death, nor contrive it soon.
Only escape, your orphanhood outrun,

Run from the glisten of those refracting egos
Where you could love and loathe yourself on sight,
To the worst priesthood, or test-tube remedy
For fratricidal passion! Run from the children
To father men and poems in your mind.

Plaint of the Poet in an Ignorant Age

I would I had a flower-boy!
I'd sit in the mid of an untamed wood
Away from tame suburbs beyond the trees.
With my botany-boy to fetch and find,
I'd sit in a rocker by a pot of cold coffee
Noodling in a notebook on my knee,
Calling, "Flower-boy, name me that flower!
Read me the tag on that tree!"
But here I sit by an unlit fire
Swizzling three martinis
While a thousand metaphors doze outdoors,
And the no-bird sings in the no-name tree.

I would I had a bug-boy
With a bug-book and a butterfly-net,
To bring me Nature in a basket of leaves:
A bug on a leaf by the goldfish bowl;
I'd sit in a rocker, a pocketful of pine-nuts
And a nutcracker knocking my knee,
Cracking nuts, jokes, and crying to my bug-boy,
"Read me the caterpillar on the leaf,
Count the number of nibbled veins
By a tree's light, in fire!"
While I, in my rocker, rolled and called,
A caterpillar crawled on the long-named leaf.

If I had a boy of Latin and Greek
In love with eleven-syllable leaves,
Hanging names like haloes on herb and shrub!

A footnote lad, a lexicon boy
Who would run in a wreath around my rocker
To kneel at my chair, at my knee
Saying, "Here is your notebook, here is your pen! —
I have found you a marvellous tree!"
But all I have is a poetry-boy,
A bottle-cap king: he cries,
Thudding from the garden, "What do you call
The no-bird that sings in the no-name tree?"

The Ungrateful Garden

Midas watched the golden crust
That formed over his streaming sores,
Hugged his agues, loved his lust,
But damned to hell the out-of-doors

Where blazing motes of sun impaled
The serried roses, metal-bright.
"Those famous flowers," Midas wailed,
"Have scorched my retina with light."

This gift, he'd thought, would gild his joys,
Silt up the waters of his grief;
His lawns a wilderness of noise,
The heavy clang of leaf on leaf.

Within, the golden cup is good
To heft, to sip the yellow mead.
Outside, in summer's rage, the rude
Gold thorn has made his fingers bleed.

"I strolled my halls in golden shift,
As ruddy as a lion's meat.
Then I rushed out to share my gift,
And golden stubble cut my feet."

Dazzled with wounds, he limped away
To climb into his golden bed.
Roses, roses can betray.
"Nature is evil," Midas said.

Promising Author

Driving on the road to Stinson Beach
I remember your witty gap-toothed face
Half-ruined in a dozen shore-leave brawls,
And the straw hair and softening gut
Of a beat-up scarecrow out of Oz.

I drove this road with you
Some sixteen years ago
Skidding on curves between the pepper trees.
You whipped the wheel as though it were a helm
And laughed at my nauseated pleas.

Once at the beach you made the finest soup
I've ever tasted: scallops, peas and leeks,
And I pictured you, the cook on some old tramp
Scudding through Conrad seas,
A boy still dazzled by his luck and grace.

Later that week, in Sausalito's
Bar with no name, I watched you curl your lip
As you ran down every writer in the place,
Unkinder with each drink,
Till I fled up the hill to the French Hotel.

After that you married Beth, so rich
She bought you monogrammed silk shirts,
A dozen at a clip,
You wore as you sneered at your shabby friends
Who had lent you money.

You became glib as any Grub Street hack,
Then demanded help
To write the novel you would never write:
As I turned you from the door
You cursed me, and I cursed you back.

Once I believed you were the great white shark,
Slick predator, with tough scarred hide.
But now I know you were a small sea-lion,
Vulnerable, whiskery, afraid,
Who wept for mercy as you died.

One to Nothing

The bibulous eagle behind me at the ball game:
"Shucks a'mighty!" coming through the rye
And Seven-Up, "I didn't mean to kick you, lady.
When you go to the Eagles' convention, you just *go!*"
Then he needles the batter from Sacramento:
"Too much ego!" he yells. "The old ego curse,
That'll hex him. The old ego never fails.
See?" he says to his phlegmatic friend,
"The bastard fanned!" And "Shucks a'mighty!"
Says again, an American from an English novel,
Named Horace or Homer, a strange colonial bird,
A raw provincial, with his outmoded slang.

"Say!" he cries to his friend, "just now I opened
One eye, saw the catcher, then the batter
In a little circle. And everything went brown.
What happened?" "*Nothing!*" says his friend.
He leans beside me, proffers the open pint.
My ego spurns him. "Fly away!" I say
To the badge on his breast. Eagle flaps down,
Confides in the man on first: "Just once a year
I have fun — see? — at the Eagles' convention.
Later I meet the other dignitaries
At the hotel. Forgive me. I'm from a small town."
He sighs, puts his head in the lap of his friend,

Listens to the portable radio, as the announcer
Makes sense of a blurry ball game
When batters turn brown, curl at the edges,
Fan and fan, like girls in early English novels,
And you can't tell the players, even with a program.
The count is two and one. We hear the *crack!*
Bat skids across the grass. The runner's on!

But eagle sleeps; he dreams away the ball game.
The dozen wasted hits, the double-plays
Are lost on him, as we lose, by one run.
Having his inning curled in a little circle,
He emerges, sucks his bottle; his badge mislaid

In the last of the ninth. We surge to the exits
While this bird claws among the peanut shells
In search of his ego. Carry him, friend,
To the dignitaries, to the eagle's ærie,
Where his mate will hone her talons on his breast.
As D. H. Lawrence wished, he has cracked the shell
Of his ego, but devoured it like a nut
Washed down with rye. And he finds oblivion
Like the lost hero of a Modern English Novel.
What happens? Nothing. Even the brilliant infield
Turns brown. Lights out. The circle fades below.
Shucks a'mighty. If you're an eagle, you just go.

The Death of a Public Servant

In Memoriam, Herbert Norman

ENVOY ACCUSED OF BEING RED KILLS SELF

Cairo, April 4, 1957 — Canadian Ambassador Herbert Norman committed suicide early today, apparently because of charges in a United States Senate subcommittee that he was a Communist. The Canadian government had denied the charges.

The embassy announced the 48-year-old career diplomat leaped from a high building. It stated he was an "extremely conscientious public servant" and that "recent unpleasant publicity and accusations greatly distressed him."

This is a day when good men die from windows,
Leap from a sill of one of the world's eyes
Into the blind and deaf-and-dumb of time;
Or by ways desperate or ludicrous
Use one of the world's machines for God's,
As George used his gun by the swimming pool
And was found in the flamingo-colored water,
Or John, drowned in a London crater,

Saw a drowned world there before he plunged:
A baby-carriage frame, a plumber's elbow,
Memorials to his dying as he died;
Now you, in Cairo, and I do not know
How that young, dedicated intellect
Was forced away at last from its long service.
Someone in Parliament says you were "killed by slander."
Wounds to your name were mortal to your mind.

Dead friends, who were the servants of this world!
Once there was a place for gentle heroes.
Now they are madmen who, scuttling down corridors,
Eluding guards, climb lavatory walls
And squeeze through air-vents to their liberation,
Where the sensitive concrete receives them
From the world's vast, abstract hate;
So they are smashed to sleep.

Or they, found wandering naked in the woods —
Numbed from the buffets of an autumn storm,
Soaked blissfully in its impersonal furies —
Are wrapped and rescued after a long dark night,
Are bustled into hospitals and baths
While the press explains away their aberrations:
"Needed a rest...and took no holidays...."
But even so, they have managed to catch their death.

I mark the fourth of April on this page,
When the sun came up and glittered on the windows
As you fell away from daylight into heaven:
The muck of Cairo, and a world silenced forever.
A poet, to whom no one cruel or imposing listens,
Disdained by senates, whispers to your dust:
Though you escape from words, whom words pursued,
Take these to your shade: of rage, of grief, of love.

Voyager

for Charles Gullans

I

Digging my claws in sand, I crawled ashore.
Children stopped their play to stare. One boy
Threw me his coat, then fled. I fell asleep
Easily, on this mild, familiar strand.
Women came running, hauled me up, then clung
Like faded pennons to my broken rigging.
Homeward they lugged the light bones of my legend.

But they were weak, and stumbled in the sand...
Did all of you journey with me in your minds,
Aged and disabled crones? At our last parting
We tumbled in the sand, and you were bitter girls
Flinging farewells at us, like pelting stones
At a retreating army. We had seemed brilliant,
Sure of our rendezvous — but you commenced our exile.

For nightmare weeks we searched our neighbor's coast
Looking to join the force that was arrayed
To march against those traitors to the Peace.
We never heard. Did they depart without us?
Did a tidal wave obliterate the camp,
The many thousand men, the tents, the stallions,
The muscled armorers hammering at the forge?

Weapons stacked beside the saffron tents
High as the ridge-pole; whole sheep on the spits
Sputtering fat that flared the fires for miles;
Camp-sounds: the creak of leather saddles, hooves
On hard-packed ground, men's curses, yapping dogs.

The cold soft voice of that great General:
Did he burn or drown? Is he in hiding now?

Wine of my province! Tasting it again
I taste my own blood, sweet when I sucked a scratch
In boyhood. Yet the aftertaste is sour,
Spoilt by an old man's breath, death in his throat.
And now I spill the cup. My hands are stiff
As a galley-slave's, and split from brine and rowing,
Smooth when I left, commander of the fleet.

II

I gave the orders that we must abandon
The search for armies that abandoned us.
Like hounds grown lean from looking, we raced back
Across the fastest, brightest autumn sea!
Sights were inaccurate: one long ribbon beach
A long mirage, seducing us from North,
Our true direction, towards a curving bay

Shaped like a siren's mouth. The Navigator
Hunted our home beyond another cove
So like the one we turned to all our lives
We feared that Heaven's hand had scooped you up,
Moved huts and livestock, children's prints in sand
Clean from the place, and set you down on grass
And daisies, in pale meadows of the dead.

We disembarked to search those teasing hills
Whose contours were familiar as our wives'.
But gradually the verdure of the slopes
Turned tropical, and we were jungle-bound.
A bird screamed like a brother; near the ground
A deadly, chuckling voice from ferns and moss.
Roots toiled our feet like snakes, became snakes.

All life voracious, fearsome, ravenous!
Great orchids dipped and gulped: and soldiers vanished
Silently, where they stood. Only the clang
Of a dropped shield on a log, or the soft hinge
Of closing flower jaws...we could not tell.
A few pulled back in time, but never whole.
As we wallowed on, we smelled our rot.

Then rain descended, not quick jungle storms
But seas upended. And the land joined in,
All elements reversing: skies dropped mud
Like excrement of Gods...and we, whipped blind
And putrid, fled to the immaculate sea.
So we believed. Staggering, caked like apes
With soil, we sensed the rains' diminishing.

Still we were puppets to the dirt. We whirled
Choking in storms of all the vast world's dust.
How many last words strangled in a cough?
We fell to the ground, to join our dust to dust.
The breeze turned sweet and whistled us awake.
We rose like the dead in vestments of white dust
But could not praise the landscape. There was none.

Only the land we stood on, like the deck
Of the universe, lost in seas of vacant space;
Laughing, with barren minds and eyes, we stared:
Scarecrow confronting scarecrow in a field
Banging our arms against our smoking sides.
And so we danced like grains of emery
Polishing the round lens of the world.

III

The Navigator fumbled at a rag
Which was a map, its rivers silted up.
We followed him till, drowning in the sand,
He said he needed water under him
To chase the stars that wriggled in the sky
Like jelly-fish. But with his closing eyes
He sighted spars, or trees, or picks for teeth....

Perspective lied: a camel was a cat.
But singing folly and mad hope aloud,
He died too soon. For if we hadn't killed him
We could have cursed him as we dragged him up
To scrape his snout over the rotten planking
Of the one remaining ship, her side stove in,
And knock his bones across that broken deck.

Despair turned lyric, and we moved like dancers:
One man fingered a rusty nail, another
Sifted a cornucopia of wheat-like sand
That overflowed the hold, and lay there humming.
For weeks, unlaboring, we watched the season alter,
Till winter fell on us like crashing armor
And the living used the dead for food and shelter.

In Spring a friendly caique picked us up.
We voyaged from isle to isle, all so alike
I could repeat one story for all. No doubt I will,
The gaffer huddled in his mouldy corner,
A bore to his descendants, mouthing lies.
So now you face the Hero, breath to breath,
And know no more than he what victory was.

1955-1964

Tying One on in Vienna

Variations on a theme of Heinrich Heine

I have been, faithfully, to the 39 birthplaces of Beethoven;
To 39 birthplaces of Beethoven have I been.
Reborn, every time, to the wrath of landladies
Who objected to the noise,
He had to move on.
Damn and bless your peripetia, Beethoven.
I am above your Meer und Stürme; I have won my haven
On high, below, in a cozy rathskeller in Vienna.

I tip the whole world down my throat,
Thirsty as Beethoven.
If I were home, I'd float on an ice cube like a polar bear
In my terrible fur, bulky as Beethoven,
Dipping my toes in an ocean of whiskey.
But here is a whole world in a golden brew:
Viennese cathedrals, where Mongol troops, I'm told,
Took pot-shots at gargoyles, to destroy their evil-eyes –
Never mind: gargoyles will rise again, gargle golden wine,
Giggle in rathskellers; Luther broke things too,
Or his followers did. Give me a golden Pope
Who wallows in artifacts, tithes a thousand villages
For one gold goblet. O I see all the Leos of all the Romes
In this glass: Agamemnon's cup, the brilliant vessels
Of Vaphio, with ruminating bulls, bulls grazing,
And bulls chased round and round the bowl by crazy Schliemann.

Turks and Hellenes, Mongols, Shakespearean scholars – Hegel!
Continuity is all!
Changing the petticoat guard at the palace of Paul;
Orange groves, All Souls' Day, 4th of July parades;
Vienna, Spokane, Los Angeles County – even Hamburg...

And over all others, the face of my lover,
A man with the brain of an angel!

Beloved, thou art fair,
With hair the color of Solomon's beard
And a big head, like Beethoven.
David the Goliath, patron saint of Florence,
Has a navel like a pigeon's swimming-pool;
You are the David of the Galleria dell'Accadèmia
Whose navel is a little golden bowl
In which I plunge my nose — Oh, what a heavenly odor!
Landlord, hold me up by the hair
Before I drown!

Der brave Mann! We sit here together
Drinking like brother and sister,
We hug each other like sister and brother
And he speaks to me of the power of love.
I drink to the health of my ex-husband
And other enemies, known and unknown.
I FORGIVE ALL LOUSY POETS
AS THEY SHALL FORGIVE ME.
I weep in an excess of feeling!

Then I cry to him, "Landlord, where are the twelve apostles,
The holy hogsheads, hidden in the back room
Where they preach to the United Nations?
Lead me to them, in their plain wooden jackets,
Looking like Mennonite farmers. Their souls are more radiant
Than the Court of St. James's, than the Fabergé eggs
In the Hermitage Museum...

Purple and Gold! My old High School colors!"
O those grand autumn days, when we crushed Immaculate Conception,
And the Society of Jesus provided cheerleaders,
Though both teams flopped down on the field to pray

Just before game-time. And I debated the girls from the convent
On, "Resolved: We should have government ownership of railroads"
And God was on my side, the affirmative.
Though I spoke with the tongue of gargoyle and angel,
God and I lost, because the girls of St. Mary's
Kept their skirts over their knees and their hands folded,
While I waved my wild hair, and bit my nails
In an excess of feeling....

Hooray! I'm being fanned by palm trees!
And the scent of orange groves in the sweet San Fernando Valley
Where I spent my childhood;
What an odor of myrrh is rising from a thousand navels!
Reel on, you rivers of the world!
Even the rathskeller door, with its broken hinges
Since the Russian troops hammered it down, looking for girls,
Even the old door, wounded with bayonet marks,
Dances and reels, and my soul staggers for joy,
And we are healed together, noble Viennese landlord!

He will steer me upstairs to the daylight,
Du braver Ratskellermeister,
And we'll see, though the gargoyles are broken,
There are angels on the roofs of the cathedral,
On all the roofs — see those angels sitting there like pigeons?
Angels of Heine and Rilke, all drunk. Singing,
Hallelujah and Yippee! If there were a sun overhead
It would be red like the nose of a drunkard,
Behind all that Viennese rain, as drunk as Beethoven
Every time he was born.
                         The soul of the world is a nose,
A nose in a navel. The red sun sets in the navel of heaven.

God save a disorderly world, and the wild United Nations!
The twelve holy hogsheads will roll forth on their keg legs
And save us all: poets, Mongolians, landlords & ladies, mad musicians.
And we'll reel on together, sing in a widening circle,
Hooray for purple and gold, for liquor and angels!

II.

PASSIONS

"But what you mean to me is dipped in blood
And tangled like the bright threads of a dream."

KUNITZ

Lovemusic

Come, freighted heart, within this port,
Bring all your bee-collected sweet,
The savor of a liberal night,
The crown of columbine, still-wet,
The muse of days. Bring your delight
To fill the palate and the plate,
To rinse the lips. Unburden, set
Your lilies on my chair of state.

Come, laden love, to this, my cave.
For here we soon may hide and move,
In havens play the courting dove,
And pace the newly-altared nave:
This vested place, this heart alive.
With fruit and wine and coupled play,
Each self will give itself away.

Come candidly, consort with me,
And spill our pleasure for a day.
Let love delay, unhurriedly,
This passing taste — I prophesy:
Remembered cinnamon and lime
Will fructify a bleaker time.

1942

Complex Autumnal

I let the smoke out of the windows
And lift the hair from my ears.
A season of birds and reaping,
A level of light appears.

Sun lies in urns on the terrace
Like the cat on the chimney. Near
Fall stirs the curtains, narrow

Ribbons of air nip my fingers.
Warm under foot, the carpet
Reminds my skin I am here.

All things begin together:
Weather and love. The ear
Hears the earth turn; we make an adjustment

To that motion: the dip of the sphere
Into autumn, and rustling music
As the leaves are shaken away. . . .

All things begin together,
Here, as I shake, at the day's
Beginning, with pleasure and fear,

Numb with night's dip and turning
When I weathered love-in-a-sphere,
Like the Siamese cat on the chimney

Mysterious, now, as a vessel,
An ark, or a precious container,
She is smoothing, sunning her fur.

I stand at the window and shiver
As the smoke wreathes out of my hair.
All things begin together:

Weather and love and fear
And the color of leaves, and pleasure.
The waxwings come to the ash trees
That rustle until they are bare.

The birds will wing from the weather
While I stand, still as the harvest,
With the sound of the fall in the air.

What the Bones Know

Remembering the past
And gloating at it now,
I know the frozen brow
And shaking sides of lust
Will dog me at my death
To catch my ghostly breath.

I think that Yeats was right,
That lust and love are one.
The body of this night
May beggar me to death,
But we are not undone
Who love with all our breath.

I know that Proust was wrong,
His wheeze: love, to survive,
Needs jealousy, and death
And lust, to make it strong
Or goose it back alive.
Proust took away my breath.

The later Yeats was right
To think of sex and death
And nothing else. Why wait
Till we are turning old?
My thoughts are hot and cold.
I do not waste my breath.

Epithalamion

You left me gasping on the shore,
A fabulous fish, all gill
And gilded scales. Such sighs we swore!
As our mirror selves
Slipped back to sea, unsundering, bumped gently there,
The room a bay, and we,
Afloat on lapping, gazes laving,
Glistered in its spume.

And all cerulean
With small, speeding clouds: the ceiling,
Lights beyond eyelids. So you reeled in me,
Reeling.

Our touch was puffed and cloudy now,
As if the most impaled and passionate thought
Was tentative in flesh.
This frail
Smile seemed, in our bodies' wash,
Like a rock-light at sea, glimmering
With all the strength of singleness in space.

Still, you will not turn aside,
Your face fallow, eyes touching.
So I cling to your tendrils of hair,
Our two tides turning
Together: towards and away
With the moon, motionless and sailing.

O my only unleaving lover,
Even in expiring, you reach again.
Thus we may rest, safe in this sealing
As beached, we lie,

Our hulks whitening, sun scaling,
While the small sea-foam dries,
And the sea recedes and the beach accedes,
Our bodies piled like casual timber
Sanded, on this pure, solar lift of hour,
Wreathed in our breathing.

We will exceed ourselves again:
Put out in storms, and pitch our wave on waves.
My soul, you will anticipate my shouting as you rise
Above me to the lunar turn of us,
As skies crack stars upon our symmetries,
Extinguished as they touch this smoky night,
And we exhale again our fume of bliss.

This is my shallow rocking to Orion:
Curling to touch the seaweed at your side.
Wrap my mermaid hair about your wrists
And seal my face upon your resinous eyes.

Foundered on finny wastes, we rest
Till dawn, a gilded layer, lies
Across the pallid sky.
The world's a tinted shell borne up where waves embrace.
Its thin, convolving valve will close and clasp
This love, so blessed:
Our sea-life, swooning as it swims, to reach
Tentacular and cleaving arms that touch
A milky flank, a drowned, reviving face.

The Patient Lovers

Love is an illness still to be,
Still away, another chill.
We shall measure mercury

Of the rising, falling will,
Of the large and resting heart,
Of the body, not quite still,

Still enough to keep the chart
From reflecting what we feel:
We shall be well, and well apart.

Still my body still will start
When from my milky side you steal,
And breathing is a casual art,

And illness we no longer play
Unless we fill the healer's part.
We will be well, and well away

Until our pulse and pallor tell
That we are ill, of being well.

Season of Lovers and Assassins

Safe from the wild storms off Cape Hatteras,
Hastily stripped, in the warm surf we embrace.

The storm we made has flung us to the sand.
A force not thought has plunged each into each.

Trailing our clothes like seaweed up the beach,
We swim to sleep, and drown, entwined in dreams.

The other ocean wakes us, where a gun
Struck, as we slept, a caring public man:

From early dawn, zoo noises bruise our ears
Played on TV's gray window to the news.

Blood fills the famous brain. The rains descend
(your gentle hands), a continent of tears.

One passionate harsh light has been put out.
Numbly we move to the noontime of our love:

The strip of rain-pocked shore gleams pallidly.
Fragments of broken palm-frond fly like knives

Through tropic wind. Soon we bear star-shaped wounds,
Stigmata of all passion-driven lives.

We leave this island, safety, to our fate,
Wrapt in a caul of vulnerability,

Marked lovers now, the moony night is ours,
Surf-sounds reminding us that good decay

Surrounds us: force which pounds on flesh or stone,
The slow assassination of the years.

June 5, 1968

On a Line from Sophocles

I see you cruel, you find me less than fair.
Too kind to keep apart, we two brutes meet.
Time, time, my friend, makes havoc everywhere.

Our stammers left to hunger in the air
Like smoke or music, turn the weather sweet:
To seek us, cruel; to find us, less than fair.

Testing our own reflections unaware
Each caught an image that was once conceit.
Time, time, my friend, makes havoc everywhere.

Eyes lewd for spotting death in life declare
That fallen flesh reveals the skull: complete.
I see you: Cruel. You find me less than fair.

The sacking of the skin, the ashen hair —
But more than surfaces compound the cheat!
Time, time, my friend, makes havoc *everywhere*

The years betray our vows to keep and care.
O traitors! ugly in this last defeat,
I find you cruel, you see me less than fair.
Time, time, my friend, makes havoc everywhere.

The Glass

Your body tolls the hour,
The hands spin round and round.
Your face, the focus of light,
Will burn me to the ground.

Losing ourselves in love
Beneath this counterpane,
Unwinding from its womb
To the all-consuming now,

All day today I die,
I die eternally,
Losing myself in joy.
By one touch you put out time.

The Light

To wake embedded in warm weight of limbs
Never till now so wholly in repose,
Then to detach your body, strand by strand
From his; but slumbering, murmurous a moment
He confidently drowns again. His arms
Gather you closer, stirring to take leave,
The birds' hushed rapture ushering the dawn.
But hesitate before you break his bonds:

Suspend this moment, see beyond the hour
His form, so tenderly alone and calm,
Yet clinging to that sensual catacomb
Where we embrace eternally in last night.
You rational marvel! As if will were all,
As if this image could be kept or doomed
By what you choose. While still he hems you round
His closed eye holds you faster than your sight.

The Gift

Gift of another day!
To hold in velvet glove
This heavy force of love,
Of you alive in me.

Gift of another noon,
Its crest of tenderness:
In touching we converse,
Thrill in our joy-spent bones.

Gift, as the light declines
Of her reviving powers.
You drench me in new wines.
I fill my hands with flowers.

Gift of another moon,
The perfect O of love
For your single arrow, bowman,
Feather and shaft and eye,

Before we are drawn away
Back into the cold
Scald of the world again
Let us rest, hold, stay.

Dangerous Games

I fly a black kite on a long string.
As I reel it in,
I see it is a tame bat.
You say it's you.

You fly a white kite, but the string snaps.
As it flutters down,
You see it is a cabbage butterfly.
I say it's I.

You invented this game,
Its terms, its terminology.
I supplied the string,
Giving you the frayed length
So I could escape.

I flew a black kite, let go the string,
But the thing darted down
Straight for my long hair
To be entangled there.

You flew a white kite that ran away,
You chased it with your bat sonar.
But you found only a cabbage butterfly
Trembling on an aphid-riddled leaf.

Heart's Limbo

I thrust my heart, in danger of decay
through lack of use,
into the freezer-compartment, deep
among the ice-cubes, rolls ready to brown 'n' serve,
the concentrated juice.

I had to remember not to diet on it.
It wasn't raspberry yoghurt.
I had to remember not to feed it to the cat
when I ran out of tuna.
I had to remember not to thaw and fry it.
The liver it resembled
lay on another shelf.

It rested there in its crystal sheath, not breathing,
preserved for posterity.

Suddenly I needed my heart in a hurry.
I offered it to you, cold and dripping,
incompletely thawed.
You didn't even wash its blood from your fingertips.
As it numbed them, you asked me to kiss your hands.
You were not even visibly frightened
when it began to throb with love.

Maimed, vicious as a ferret mutilated
by an iron trap set for bigger game,
dangerous, smooth as a young stone-bathing serpent,
nude, vulnerable as a new-hatched bird,
now my heart rests in your warm fingers' cage.

Console and heal my heart with gentleness.
Quicken its beat with your caresses.
Be passionate! Be bold!
Give me your heart to hold.

Winter Song

on a line from Arthur Waley

So I go on, tediously on and on....
We are separated, finally, not by death but life.
We cling to the dead, but the living break away.

On my birthday, the waxwings arrive in the garden,
Strip the trees bare as my barren heart.
I put out suet and bread for December birds:
Hung from evergreen branches, greasy gray
Ornaments for the rites of the winter solstice.

How can you and I meet face to face
After our triumphant love?
After our failure?

Since this isolation, it is always cold.
My clothes don't fit. My hair refuses to obey.
And, for the first time, I permit
These little anarchies of flesh and object.
Together, they flick me towards some final defeat.

Thinking of you, I am suddenly old....
A mute spectator as the months wind by.
I have tried to put you out of my mind forever.

Home isn't here. It went away with you,
Disappearing in the space of a breath,
In the time one takes to open a foreknown letter.
My fists are bruised from beating on the ground.
There are clouds between me and the watery light.

Truly, I try to flourish, to find pleasure
Without an endless reference to you
Who made the days and years seem worth enduring.

Streets of Pearl and Gold

> *Tis not what it once was, the World;*
> *But a rude heap together hurl'd....*
> ANDREW MARVELL

I

Within, walls white as canvas stretched to stain;
A tabula rasa clean as a stripped bed.
The painter's order: jars and brushes neat,
Harmoniously fixed, like palette clots.
Here, perilous in this secret nest, he paces,
Naked and fierce, dressed only in his paint;
His place condemned, pinched nearer by the beast,
The lover streaked with motley, seeing white,
Would cuff the ball and hammer with his fist
But hides instead, frowns, grappling with art:
Waves and flames and clouds and wounds and rags.
While I sit careless on the bed; I float
Posing as Venus in a pearly boat.
How wide we dream! His picturing and mine,
As the light glitters, deepening our breath
Until we sink for pearls through profound seas,
Swimming before the funeral of the earth.

II

Outside, the buildings kneel as if yielding up
To the levelers their infirm confessions:
Not rats or roaches in the wainscot
Nor the old staled odors of man's functioning
But that they were chalice of our history,
And this, a pastoral Dutch village. Here
In a black-shuttered tavern, clarks and squires

In linsey-woolsey, plotted revolution!

Yea, the streets were steep with mud and dung
From which we raised ourselves a dwelling-place,
On sober frames affixed a frontispiece.
Later, these first buildings failed in form
When they admitted to their broken cells
Child-sweat and chilblain, women laboring
Hook-shouldered, early deformed by the machine:
A house of light become a cave of pain.

Now cornice, fretwork, sagging pediment,
Outliving purity and sin, each warrant signed,
Tell more than Bowery faces of our fate.
The stain is mortal on their livid meat,
Emptier than this periled wood and stone.
A lover carved here, priding in his skill,
Above the old eye-levels, garland, gargoyle,
In the time of the artisan, when our land was small.

III

Sun dust. Noon is noiseless. Stink of fish
From Fulton, all the produce gone by ten
Save for squashed jelly, viscid scales
Rusting and iridescent. Seasoning sprinkled
On the cooked street.

A wino crawls onto a briny tray,
Lies down in inches of left-over sea.
Curling, crustacean-red, he dozes
                              his non-death away.

Nearby, the pier where we watch trawlers:
Mending their nets, men sweat, look up, scowl, smile;
Held still a moment, beetles caught in crystal.
The River is brown jelly in the sun.

Between the air and water flies the Bridge:
The twang of her long azure strings...
Below us, grass grows over boards and water;
AMERICA, THE DEAD IN CHRIST RISE FIRST
On bulkheads scrawled unevenly, fuzzing chalk
Xs in rows, the childlike mark of love.

IV

Retreat to darkness, two dark flights away!
Tin ceilings, thinly blue: pale rippling.
All afternoon the water undulates...

The sky is silent. For the wino in the tray.
He has not moved, or died.

We rouse in the opal twilight, open eyes:
Dust, a marble crust ground underfoot;
Splintering sills crumble, frame the street
Laid like a whip across the backs of blasted lots
Near rubble mountains raised by dying men.

Bits of the old town lean on the August air,
Wait blindly for the X of the builder-killers,
Their multitudinous eyes taped out.

Racks of white crosses fenestrate the night,
Before the two hairs cross in the last bomb-sight.

And who are we, for whom our country cares?
America makes crosses of us all.
Each artist in his fortress: boiling oil
A weapon still. Seething across his canvases, a fury
Flung over white, ripped out: the X in paint.

V

Art is this marveling fury of spurned love.
Caught in this present, impatient of histories,
Even your own, while you mourn what vanishes.
Who endures, rootless? But our roots are strewn
On every pavement, smashed or drowned in brine.

Observe the world with desperate affection;
Snatch up your brush to catch it, fix it all
On canvases which, stacked against a wall,
Dozen on dozen, are crumbling unseen.
Paint out the day and you will keep the time:

Exhaust fumes, and a building's trembling dust,
Fish entrails, wino-reek, attic waste,
The shapes below the names on billboard signs,
And — what the bums find early — paint the dirt
Which we all come to: paint the old dirt sleep.

So stamp your canvas with the X of loss,
Art mutilated, stained with abuse and rage.
But mark it also as the cross of love
Who hold this woman-flesh, touch it alive,
As I try to keep us, here upon the page.

III.

FATHER

Thrall

The room is sparsely furnished:
A chair, a table and a father.

He sits in the chair by the window.
There are books on the table.
The time is always just past lunch.

You tiptoe past as he eats his apple
And reads. He looks up, angry.
He has heard your asthmatic breathing.

He will read for years without looking up
Until your childhood is over:

Smells, untidiness and boring questions;
Blood, from the first skinned knees
To the first stained thighs;
The foolish tears of adolescent love.

One day he looks up, pleased
At the finished product.
Now he is ready to love you!

So he coaxes you in the voice reserved
For reading Keats. You agree to everything.

Drilled in silence and duty,
You will give him no cause for reproach.
He will boast of you to strangers.

When the afternoon is older
Shadows in a smaller room
Fall on the bed, the books, the father.

You read aloud to him
"La Belle Dame sans Merci."
You feed him his medicine.
You tell him you love him.

You wait for his eyes to close at last
So you may write this poem.

My Good Father

PIERONE'S INC.

RIVERSIDE AND POST — SPOKANE, WASHINGTON 99201

to: Carolyn Kizer
1401 LeRoy Avenue
Berkeley, California 94708

Dear Carolyn:

I'm attempting to put together a Study Club paper on the subject of your father Ben. I make no bones about my literary abilities, but he has long fascinated me, and at least one benefit of the paper will fall to me: some of my curiosities about him may be satisfied.

My sources will be those enormous files your lawyer laid in my office, the *Review-Chronicle* files on him, and some local interviewing.

But I need some insights that the above cannot provide. I want to know more intimate facts about him. He came across as supremely structured, intelligent, polite but always somewhat remote. What was he like to you? How close could he or would he get, was he tactile, did he understand you? Did he have any fears about himself? Was he as strong as he appeared? Was he a loving husband?

Whatever is convenient and comfortable for you to send I'll appreciate.

Bob Pierone

MEN'S CLOTHING, FURNISHINGS AND SPORTSWEAR
FEATURING HICKEY-FREEMAN

KIZER, BENJAMIN HAMILTON, lawyer; b. Champaign County, Ohio, Oct. 29, 1878; s., Benjamin Franklin and Mary Louise (Hamilton) K.; LL.B., U. Mich., 1902; LL.D., Linfield Coll., McMinnville, Oreg., Reed Coll., Portland, Oreg.; m. Helen Bullis, May 19, 1915 (dec. Sept. 1919); m. 2d Mabel Ashley, Mar. 12, 1921 (dec. Oct. 1955); 1 dau., Carolyn Ashley (Mrs. John Marshall Woodbridge). Admitted to Mich. bar, 1902, Wash. bar, 1902, U.S. Supreme Ct. bar, 1936; practice in Spokane, 1902 – ; spl. master U.S. Circuit Ct. Appeals, 9th Circuit, 1942-44; dir. China Office, UNRRA, 1944-46; Walker-Ames prof. internat. relations U. Wash., 1946-47, Pres. Spokane City Plan Commn. 1928-44; chmn. Wash. Planning Council, 1933-44; chmn. Pacific N. W. Regional Planning Commn.; former pres. Am. Soc. Planning Ofcls.; chmn. World Affairs Council of Inland Empire. Assoc.; chmn. W. coast lumber commn. Nat. War Labor Bd.; Wash. Chmn. Crusade for Freedom 1950; chmn. Rhodes Scholars Exam. Com. for 6 Pacific N. W. States 1932-64. Bd. regents Reed Coll. Portland. Recipient Auspicious Star, Grand Cordon (China). Mem. Am. Wash. (past pres.), Spokane County (past pres.) bar assns. Phi Beta Kappa, Order of Coif. Author: The U.S. Canadian Northwest. Home: Culmstock Arms Apts., Spokane WA 99201.

(Benjamin Kizer died on April 8, 1978, in his 100th year.)

Dear Bob,

I'm glad to sit down and think about the questions you asked in your letter about Dad. They were the kind a good biographer would be concerned with. "Supremely structured, intelligent, polite but always somewhat remote," you said. So he appeared to all but his intimates. Add "authoritarian and severe," and you get a pretty close approximation of how he appeared to that stranger, his child. After his death, his long-time secretary told me that for about the first six years of my life he referred to me as "Mabel's baby," a rather unusual parthenogenetic attitude! Despite having a younger brother and sister, he seemed to view me much as an early Renaissance painter saw a child: as an adult in miniature. One was expected to be a wholly rational person: no tantrums, no tears, no noisy outbursts whether of shouting, laughing or sneezing! As a father, you'll appreciate that this attitude was, to say the least, unrealistic. And for a number of years it obscured for me the fact that he was the most loving, demonstrative and affectionate husband and father.

Two things should be remembered: first, that he was nearly 50 when I was born. He required – demanded – a tranquil household, where nothing should be permitted to disturb his constant activity of thinking and reading. Second, he hadn't had much of a childhood himself. As a small boy on the farm in Ohio, he was expected to work, like everyone else. And when he came to Spokane, still a child, the death of his father required him to leave school and work again: selling newspapers on the streets of Spokane, to support his mother, brother and sister. A forced maturity then, at least a decade before anyone of our generation was expected to behave like an adult. Only the most rigorous self-discipline saw him through this terrible period. (Of this, and the price he paid for it, more anon.)

Partly as a result of his attitude towards me, I learned to write and read as early as humanly possible. Then, my going to school, and learning things, and getting good marks, began to give us something in common. He was very conscientious about doing things with me during these years (whether prodded by my mother or not, I do not know): taking me for walks and talks (I was expected to discuss intelligently recent Supreme Court decisions at around the age of eight or so), learning to ice skate with me, buying me a bike, going on picnics and expeditions into the country — all activities which I think he genuinely enjoyed. My fear of him diminished, but didn't altogether evaporate until I was around 30 and he was around eighty. Disciplining me was pathetically easy: all he needed to do was speak my name, in what I later discovered was his courtroom voice, and I was quelled. Of course, communication between us was still imperfect. I remember the time in my childhood when he was angriest with me. Like many episodes in the rocky history of parent-child relations, this one grew out of a misunderstanding. During Hoover's first campaign, both of my parents were enthusiastic; my mother, in particular, worked very hard for his election. They were soon disillusioned. Because we were an intensely political household, I was quite aware of this. It was borne in upon me that the name "Roosevelt" was being bruited about in accents of mingled doubt and hope. I knew that Roosevelt was a Democrat, that we had been Republicans, and that we were changing sides. In the middle of a dinner party, with interesting out-of-town guests, one of them asked if we were Democrats or Republicans. "Oh," I interjected breezily, "we veer with the wind." Now at the age of seven or so, precocious as I undoubtedly was (precocity was a survival trait in my relations with my father), I had no idea of the negative implications of this phrase, which indeed I found pleasant and expressive. My father was livid. I have suppressed what he said, but I know that I withered like a violet in an ice-storm.

This little episode also illustrates what was wrong with my upbringing in another respect: Like all bright only children of elderly parents, I was expected to provide the floor-show for visitors. And, like all children, I was thrilled by praise, and tried to top myself: louder, if not funnier. Suddenly the petted and exploited one heard the voice of thunder, and saw the long, bony finger of doom. I assure you, this is not just a writer's hyperbole. If there are still any among those present who were ever on the wrong side of my father in a courtroom, they will recall, all too vividly, what a viscera-shrivelling experience it could be. With no prior warning, the kind and indulgent father could turn in an instant into the terror of the courtroom. A verbally battered child, I never knew what hit me. In later life, when I saw the same treatment meted out to members of the House Un-American Activities Committee and other villains of the '50s, to even more devastating effect, I almost forgave him.

I remember, in his early nineties he said an extraordinary thing to me: "The last thing we learn about ourselves is our effect." I think this remark well illustrates his special genius. How he affected others may have been one of the last things he learned, but he went on trying.

Husbandhood is perhaps the finest example of how, in him, the conscious learning-process went on, almost until the end. My mother, until she met my father in her mid-forties, had had a difficult and damaging life. Curiously — or perhaps not so curiously — my Grandfather Ashley was very like my father. A figure cold, austere and frightening to his children, and seen as kind and indulgent only later. Unfortunately my mother did not have the shelter I did. She lost her own mother when she was barely entering adolescence, and soon acquired the proverbially cruel step-mother. (I have no idea what this lady was like in reality.) While finishing her own schooling (a Ph.D. in Biology from Stanford in 1904 — pretty unusual for a woman in those days, even in these), and for long years afterwards, she was making a major financial contribution to the education of her younger brothers and step-brothers. She worked, worked, worked, at a variety of fascinating jobs, which I will forbear from describing as this is his story, not hers. Politically, she was a radical, and sexually she was liberated, but alas, I fear, not liberated enough not to feel guilty. Not too many years before she met my father — she was forty — she had a devastating love affair with a fascinating, worldly and eminent man of the Hemingway *macho* type. From this, she declined into tuberculosis, as so many women before her have done. Tuberculosis! That great escape-hatch. How do we get along without it?

So I think it must have been a weary and chastened lady who collapsed into my father's arms, on a bench on the mezzanine of the

65

Davenport Hotel, just two weeks after they had met, and agreed to marry him. (In later years, we would make short, sentimental pilgrimages to that bench. Daddy used to joke with Mr. Davenport about buying it.) My father always claimed that he fell in love with her over the telephone, before he ever saw her. "Her voice was ever soft, / Gentle and low, an excellent thing in woman," he would quote again and again, with never-diminishing pleasure. For Daddy, if a thing was good, it stayed good. His middle name was fidelity.

Periodically, during their marriage, I heard the oft-repeated refrain, "If only we had met twenty years earlier!" Then they would variously collapse in ruefulness and laughter, one voice or the other confessing that, in youth, they had been far too willful and stubborn to have made a go of it. But life had taught a great deal to both of them, supremely intelligent as they both were. Hard lessons, harsh lessons, absorbed in loss and pain.

Unlike mother, father had been married before. At the age of thirty-six, he began writing fan letters to Helen Bullis, then the poetry critic for the *New York Times Book Review*. Helen was a confirmed spinster, seven years older than he, devoted to her aging and crippled mother, with all thought of matrimony, if it had ever entered her mind, put well behind her. On the strength of a handful of letters and a snapshot, father proposed. Incredulous, Helen disposed. Father bided his time. In due course, Helen wrote him that her mother was desperately ill. Father hopped on a train for New York. He arrived just in time to catch the body, so to speak. He comforted the bereaved, took care of all the funeral arrangements with wonderful competence I'm sure, and generally made himself useful, if not indispensable. Poor Helen never had a chance. Triumphantly, he returned to Spokane with his captured bride. From his standpoint, it was a long honeymoon, terminated by Helen's death, only four years and four months later.

They had a mutual joy in horseback riding. One day, Helen's horse puffed out his belly when the saddle was being cinched; later, the saddle slipped under the horse, and he kicked her to death before my father could reach them. Ben was absolutely devastated. To tell how devastated, I need only mention that he, most rational of men, dabbled in spiritualism for awhile, finally to turn in disgust

66

from its palpable charlatanry. From the autumn of 1919 to the harsh spring of 1921, my father was a man in mourning, a man whose brightening prospects had turned to the dark night of the soul. It was the thought of this bereaved, forsaken man that prompted Norman Coleman, President of Reed College, to suggest to my mother that she phone Ben Kizer when she visited Spokane in the course of her work.

Let's pause for a moment, and consider Mr. Rational, as you, and I, knew him. How impulsive can one get? To propose to a woman never seen nor spoken to; and to another, whose voice one fell for over the telephone, a scant two weeks after meeting! And, in both cases, to be supremely right. To love both women with a passion that never diminished, never faded. Consider further: Both these handsome, intelligent, intellectual women were into their forties. Now we must return, for a moment, to that little boy selling newspapers. By his account, young Ben used to rouse himself at four a.m., so that he might gather up his early edition of the paper and haunt the entrances of the saloons and whorehouses, where the emerging customers, genial and loaded, might carelessly toss a dollar to a little boy instead of the expected nickel. Now we all know, by hearsay and reading, what a tough little frontier town Spokane was in the '80s, a hundred years ago. Its primary purpose was to service the loggers and miners come to town on a toot, to rake the money from their burning pockets by whatever means. When Daddy would tell of those days as a poor newsie, counting every penny that he brought home to pour into his devout Methodist mother's lap, I'd recall those lines of Blake:

> But most through midnight streets I hear
> How the youthful harlot's curse
> Blasts the new-born infant's tear,
> And blights with plagues the marriage hearse.

What was blighted in Ben, and kept him a virgin until 37, was the notion that the flesh alone, prettiness alone, soiled and profaned as it was by need and booze and money, was not enough for him. That the fastidious young puritan could grow into a mature man who positively revelled in sexual love, is a minor miracle.

But what about "nice girls" in Spokane? Like the kind his brother married: nice, respectable, unread and rather stupid. No, for Ben it had to be everything. He never betrayed a flicker of interest in beautiful dumb women. But I'm afraid he never had any interest in homely intelligent ones either! In my memory, the two women who really turned him on were Mme. Pandit, sister of Nehru, and Mme. Sun Yat Sen, both ladies well along in life, both beautiful and diamond-bright. If required to choose between the company of women and that of men, he would unhesitatingly choose the former.

In his eighties, he became pally with some of the nuns at Fort Wright College of the Holy Names. I came to visit him one time when he was still bubbling with pleasure over an evening he had just spent there. Mother Superior, knowing how he detested amateur performances of any kind (to the extent that he never attended any musical or dramatic event at school in which I took part), had assured him that the young woman pianist who was to perform was indeed exceptional. And indeed she had been. It seemed there had been a party afterwards, at which he'd clearly had a wonderful time.

"How many people were there, Daddy?" I inquired.

"Oh, about forty, I guess."

"And how many other men?"

"Hm..." He thought for awhile. "I guess...there weren't *any!*"

He hadn't noticed. His total absence of what we now call 'sexism' was one of the qualities for which I cherished him.

In case I'm making Ben sound a little too good to be true, I hasten to add that he was an undoubted "leg man." How he loathed the advent of slacks and jeans! He could not refrain from moans and sighs when I and his granddaughters lounged around in these convenient garments. And what joy he took in the mini-skirt! His nurses told me that, well into his nineties, when a young lady visited him wearing a scrap of skirt that barely cleared her crotch, he was riveted to the spot. He and his heroes, Oliver Wendell Holmes and Benjamin Franklin, had a lot more in common than what went on upstairs.

But to get back to Ben and that wounded bird of passage, my

mother (who, incidentally, had great legs): How tenderly he watched over her, alert to the slightest nuance that would indicate that her perpetual self-dissatisfaction had gained the upper hand! How he lavished praise on her, discriminating praise that she could not turn aside, as she habitually did when complimented by outsiders! And he found something to praise in her, something with which to cajole or please her, *every day* of their married life of thirty-four years. Oh, they quarreled, hotly. Mother would rush to the bedroom and shut the door. When he'd cooled down, Ben would compose a note, and slip it under the door. Sullen, reluctant, mother would emerge. But he noticed that she'd put on lipstick and smoothed her hair. A little tease, a little hug, and a smile would break through the mask, unwilling at first, then radiant and whole-hearted. Mother told me that my father was always the first to patch up a quarrel, that the sun was never permitted to go down upon her wrath, or his. He was a wonderful husband, and she freely admitted it. Whether or not she was ever "in love" with him remains a question. And it's not a question to which children can give an authoritative answer. I know she believed him to be the finest man in all her not inconsiderable experience. And I have to agree with that. I never knew him to have a venal or self-serving moment. I never heard him tell a fib, much less a lie — to himself, or to anyone else. He was, in an old-fashioned phrase which I cherish because of him, "the soul of honor."

He was a man who performed numberless acts of charity and generosity without the necessity of telling anyone about them. Mother and I found out only by accident, and there must be thousands of incidents known only to him and the recipient of his kindness. And he knew how to perform an act of charity without shame to the recipient. Once, when he was in his eighties, I wandered into his law office, to find him confronted by an Italian matriarch, in rusty black, obviously creaking with poverty and age. Something about water rights, which he had settled to her obvious relief. Dad waved me to the chair. Suddenly, anxiety was chasing gratitude right off her old, creased face. "And-a what do I owe-a you, Meester Kizer?" she asked, clutching her old cracked leather coin purse.

Daddy put the tips of his fingers together and took it under advisement. "Well, Mrs. Giovanni," he said, courteous as always, "I'm afraid I'll have to charge you twenty cents." Relief flooded her face. With fingers as cracked as her wallet, she extracted two dimes, which he gravely accepted, and proceeded to enter in his little black book. We shook hands all around, and Dad and I sailed out to lunch

Faults? Of course. With the exceptions noted above, of his concern for my mother and other needy people, he was the most self absorbed — call it "narcissistic" if you will, if that quality can be present without a trace of vanity about his exterior person — human being that I have ever known. He didn't have to tell anyone of his good deeds because the only person whose exorbitantly high standards he had to satisfy was himself. He was absolutely — and I mean absolutely — indifferent to what people thought of him. He knew that people smiled when he walked downtown in the rain wearing a woman's plastic babushka on his enormous head (no hat would fit it). He simply didn't give a curse. Allied to this indifference was that he was perfectly secure in his masculinity. I think this must be attributed to a mother who uncritically adored him and a sister who idolized him (and who was lost to him when she died early, in childbirth, to his evergreen sorrow). That's not enough to explain it, of course, but it's the best I can do.

I think, if the truth must be told, he didn't care very much for very many people. He deeply loved a few men friends, and needless to say, outlived them all: Norman Coleman, George Greenwood, Joel Ferris, Connor Malott, Richard Hargreaves, Stanley Webster, Bishop Cross — nearly all of them members of the Study Club. But for several generations this town was full of people who idolized him, whose names he could barely remember, and quickly forgot.

To him, people were chiefly important as vehicles by which he could express his passion for abstractions, abstractions for which he gaily marched into battle, chanting his war chant: truth, justice, equity, freedom and law. How he loved the law! Until his infirmities overcame him, I believe he was a truly happy man. But I don't want to leave him in his bed, at the end — a bed that never knew the print of his body in the daytime until he was over 93. I want to go back in time about 90 years. It's five o'clock in the morning, and a skinny, undernourished little newsboy is pushing a paper at you: "All about the death...Getcher paper here mister! All about the death of Charles Stewart *Parnell*!"

All the best to you and the Study Club,

Carolyn

Antique Father

there is something
        you want urgently
                to communicate
                        to me

it is in your eyes
        of ancient
                glacier water

I wait
        I try to listen
                try to tolerate
your terrible silence

                speak   Father

I believe you believe
        I am ready

                we are both tense
I with expectancy
        and the terror you once
                inspired in me

quelling all queries
        of my childhood

not the terror with which we
        (I over your shoulder)
                gaze into the pit
eternity

                        Father speak
from the last edge
                where all folly
                        become wisdom
becomes folly again

                self-quelled   I listen
                        but the lesson
is your nervous silence
                alone on the edge
more than you want to tell
                        you don't want
                                to tell
your grave secret

                stern and reticent
                        you cannot say
that I cannot know

                now will never know
                        if you ever knew

IV.

FRIENDS

Amusing Our Daughters

for Robert Creeley

We don't lack people here on the Northern coast,
But they are people one meets, not people one cares for.
So I bundle my daughters into the car
And with my brother poets, go to visit you, brother.

Here come your guests! A swarm of strangers and children;
But the strangers write verses, the children are daughters like yours.
We bed down on mattresses, cots, roll up on the floor:
Outside, burly old fruit trees in mist and rain;
In every room, bundles asleep like larvæ.

We waken and count our daughters. Otherwise, nothing happens.
You feed them sweet rolls and melon, drive them all to the zoo;
Patiently, patiently, ever the father, you answer their questions.
Later we eat again, drink, listen to poems.
Nothing occurs, though we are aware you have three daughters
Who last year had four. But even death becomes part of our ease:
Poems, parenthood, sorrow, all we have learned
From these, of tenderness, holds us together
In the center of life, entertaining daughters
By firelight, with cake and songs.

You, my brother, are a good and violent drinker,
Good at reciting short-line or long-line poems.
In time we will lose all our daughters, you and I,
Be temperate, venerable, content to stay in one place,
Sending our messages over the mountains and waters.

after Po chü-I

The Way We Write Letters

for Robert Peterson

We must lie long in the weeds
in places like Palo Alto or Perugia,
get lost to find ourselves, get going *soon*.
But none of the old Hearth & Home;
be a Dugan or Creeley, all arrowheads
and .22 cartridges studded and strewn inside,
find new places to rest and nest. Get looser;
get back to (you said) daytime drinking, mu-
sic of Telemann, Schütz, Buxtehude.
Don't keep your house in order.
If you have any further suggestions for
improving chaos, please write or wire.

We should lie long in the woods, full of light.
Old friends get published again, though losing
their moon & vinegar. Write me soon (I said).
Meanwhile, find a new place too,
where air, not character, is cool.
Not Sausalito. San Gimignano?
There, despite psychiatry, towers simply *are*
in a piercing, lyric, prodigal confusion,
regulated. Well, remember Heller in Paradise.
Madness & you (we both said). Stay sane and annoyed,
drunk in the daytime. Call your book, *Home for the Night*.
But don't go home tomorrow. Write me instead
from the meadow. Turn on the poem & the light.

Love Song

for Ruthven Todd

O to fall easily, easily, easily in Love
As nursling birds tumble from the nest
(not – pray – into the dog's jaws).
True lovers of women tend to love
Not grossly, but in gross lots
("Without deduction for tare, tret or waste,"
Webster says), love every look,
Think each new taste the best.

O to fall in Love, easily, easily
As a mild child falls to, at the breast
(not as an iron-jawed child clamps on),
To inhale all sweet ambience, breezily
Exhale flowered breath
While rapturously curls the pillowed fist,
Toes clenched in comfort,
Each new taste the best.

O Love, easily, easily, easily to fall
As fledgling bird or child is lost
(within a plot, not acres away),
Only to turn around, and find the haven
That has not moved at all.
Learn lose-and-find without much cost,
Terror smoothed in feathered, ruffled bosom,
And easily, Love, easily to rest.

Horseback

for Raymond Carver

Never afraid of those huge creatures
I sat sky-high in my western saddle
As we roared through the woods of skinny pine;
The clump clump of his great delicate hooves
Stirring plumes of pine-needle-scented dust!
One casual hand on the pommel,
The other plunged in the red coarse hair of his mane.

I remember the day he stopped dead on the trail
Trembling all over. We smelt bear, then heard
The chattering song of the rattler.
My hypnotised bay couldn't move. Time stopped:
The burnt odor of sage, the smoky noon air
And the old old snake, as big around as my skinny wrist,
Rising up from his rock.

Then the screen goes blank, and next it's summer camp:
I've mastered a wild mare bare-back, whipping one arm
In sky-wide circles like a movie cowboy,
Screaming with joy.
So now when a stubborn skittery horse runs away with me
I give him his head. But as he tries to skin me off,
Plunging under low branches, I grit, "Oh no you don't!"

I bury my face in his neck, hang on for dear life,
Furious, happy, as he turns to race for home.
We pound into the stable yard and I dismount,
But wonder at curious glances turned my way
Until I see myself in the tack-room mirror,
My face a solid mass of purple welts.
Then I begin to sneeze and sneeze. My allergies

Burst into bloom, and I am forced to quit,
And don't sit a mount again for twenty years
Until I get to Pakistan
And Brigadier Effendi puts me up
On his perfect white Arab mare.
My thighs tighten the old way as I marry a horse again...
I just wanted to tell you about it, Ray.

Linked Verses

for Donald Keene

Read a thousand books!
Consult your dreams! Drink spirits.
Then write your poem.

The poet, tossing pebbles,
Muses on rings within rings.

When the rains descend,
Life, that was buried forever,
Sends up a cool green flame.

What is as new as a toad!
The unborn calls to the born.

Pricked on the furze-bush,
You reached for the kindling axe
And forgot the blossom.

So rough, they catch on the silk,
How shall my hands keep busy?

Gold chrysanthemums
Have the faint, acrid odor
Of Mortality.

Pain, ugliness, old age:
At least they make no demands.

The frost was late this year:
Crystal nips the petals,
As my lover grows impatient.

The blind worm says to his brother,
"Who will need us when we die?"

The Good Author

for Barnard Malamud

Contrary to the views
A few days earlier
Of a fading Irish poet
Who flared into the room
With Rimbaud round his shoulder
But with hair and spirit
Receding, too much the wise
Predator not to know it,
You told us to be good.
Meaning: pure in spirit,
To strive for purity.
"Oh, play as much as you like!
But remember that an author
Is one who labors daily
Putting words to paper,
Not a man who wrote a book,"
You concluded, quietly, gravely.

We were aware as we walked
Through the campus in the snow
Of a game of hare and hound:
We found him chasing her
In tighter and tighter circles,
The innocent one flying
From wily nose and jaws.
Then he cracked the diameter,
And the only rule she knew,
To plunge her to the ground.

We could not save her, nor
Quickly enough turn away,
Fists over ears, lids clenched
From the brilliant agony.
And now your calm tones linger,
But tinctured with her cry.
Though I shall not wed the image
To any word you say.

From an Artist's House

for Morris Graves

I

A bundle of twigs
On the roof. We study pictures:
Nests of hern and crane.
The artist who built this house
Arranged the branches there.

II

Is the inlaid box
With a gilt hasp concealing
A letter, a jewel?
Within, a bunch of feathers,
The small bones of a bird.

III

The great gold kakemono
With marvelous tapes and tassels,
Handles of pale bone,
Is a blaze on the wall. Someone
Pinned an oak-leaf to the silk.

IV

Full of withered oranges,
The old, lopsided compote
Reposes on the sill.
Poor crockery, immortal
On twenty sheets of paper.

Reading Your Poems in Your House
While You Are Away

for Richard Shelton

This morning my first roadrunner
paused on the dry wall you built
right outside your window.
A couple of playful jackrabbits
bounded among the cactus
under a chilly sun.

The mountains are mirage-like
as if they had just leaked
from one of your poems
and the god over there
had puffed them full of air
to float on a blur of sage
and desert broom.

Insubstantial mountains!
I found their serious weight
inside your books.
I found the serious roadrunner
not cartoon-like at all
with a tail full of adverbs.

I follow the dry wall
as it twists from page to page,
the glowing yellow stones
spontaneous but neat
nested together, held by your sweat;
rabbits, your cactus garden,
saguaro, living tombstones on the lawns;

dogs that serially howled at dawn,
your big white dog — when a coyote screamed.
And the bitter dark.

You remember I told you
after our night on the desert
I never see the first full moon
without thinking of you?

And your perfect poem about history:
How do you like nesting
in someone else's life?

Remember this when you come home:
One day, as you pause in composing,
a phrase of mine will leap into your stanza.
Just as, in writing this,
I borrow the words that belong to you
and give them back, like moonlight.

A Poet's Household

Three for Theodore Roethke

The stout poet tiptoes
On the lawn. Surprisingly limber
In his thick sweater
Like a middle-aged burglar.
Is the young robin injured?

She bends to feed the geese
Revealing the neck's white curve
Below her coiled hair.
Her husband seems not to watch,
But she shimmers in his poem.

A hush is on the house,
The only noise, a fern
Rustling in a vase.
On the porch, the fierce poet
Is chanting words to himself.

To an Unknown Poet

I haven't the heart to say
you are not welcome here.
Your clothes smell of poverty, illness
and unswept closets.
You come unannounced to my door
with your wild-faced wife and your many children.
I tell you I am busy.
I have a dentist's appointment.
I have a terrible cold.
The children would run mad
through our living room, with its collected
bibelots and objects of art.
I'm not as young as I was.
I am terrified of breakage.

It's not that I won't help you.
I'd love to send you a box
of hand-milled soap;
perhaps a check,
though it won't be enough to help.
Keep in mind that I came to your reading:
Three of us in the audience,
your wife, myself, and the book-store owner,
unless we count the children who played trains
over your wife's knees in their torn jeans
and had to be hushed and hushed.

Next month I am getting an award
from the American Academy
and Institute of Arts and Letters.
The invitation came on hand-laid paper
thick as clotted cream.

I will travel by taxi
to 156th Street, where the noble old building,
as pale as the Acropolis,
is awash in a sea of slums.
And you will be far away, on the other coast,
as far from our thoughts as Rimbaud
with his boy's face and broken teeth,
while we eat and drink and congratulate each other
in this bastion of culture.

Two Poets by the Lake

for James Wright

I

Here lake-shore modulated to a cove;
Mud-hens, ducks and grebes came coasting near our hands.
A few aggressive gulls snatched at stale loaves
We had not yet broken, drove the others back
As we cast our bread on February waters.

You had turned away from the chrome-trimmed car,
The too-neat frozen lawns across the street;
Mail-box and fire-plug on the parking strip
Like squat fraternal twins, regarding us.

Pale with cold, and the forcing of emotion,
You shook off chrome, and crumbs, the century,
And bade me enter your chill pastoral.

You failed, I failed. We fed the waterfowl,
Stayed as we came, shaken, disconsolate,
In hope that something further might be said,
It was told now, a cold story, unresolved;
The raw scream of a gull ripped the sky's gray caul.

Vacuous, I gazed into the lake
Reflecting various vain waterfowl
As I could not, would not, mirror you.
How the vapor of your voice rose overhead!

The word made visible, a trance, an ectoplasm,
A sign, in smoke, to the sceptical believer
Who said, "It's no use, Tom. Let's go on home."

What a bucolic poem you wrote then!
Post-box and plug were gone; a moderate season;
A country lake, not town. The selective artist
Erased gulls, mallards, coots and candy-wrappers,
Laid bedding grass upon the muddy shore.

We lie down side by side, are lost in love
Instead of simply lost. We go home to each other:
And so, fulfilled, though time and place are gone,
Though we have not touched, except on paper.

Do you still look for the lady of the lake?
Or walk, waist-deep, into the quaking waters,
Fracturing your reflection as you go?

III

I add a coda to your poem here:
Where we paraded our rapt self-dismay,
Muffled and breathy, numb-lipped and morose,
Wildlife has fled. No more
Articulate doubts and mouldy crusts of bread.

A hydroplane has sliced across your voice;
The passive, silvery bay, churned to morass.
Pits have been dug, where the wide-backed hulls
Nest before racing, bed in grease and noise.

Then, summoned to the starting line,
Take off like a pack of bloodhounds baying
Each time the hulls hit water as they fly

Past shoals of bystanders, tireless and morbid, waiting
By our shallows, for a death or agony.

They face, as we did not, a final mating:
Boat slams into boat, buoy or debris.
A cushion, or a sodden book of verse
One drunken lover drops from his canoe
Can toss three thousand horses. Fatality!

Now raw, but moribund, in this mid-winter,
Still the deserted pits, the barren bank
Represent a violent coming-together,
Given the man, the water, the event.

While we are true neither to life nor nature,
But perhaps to one another as we write:
Your sensuous pastoral, or my murky weather,
The laying of the past, line upon line.
The baulked need urgent in your words, and mine.

Final Meeting

Old friend, I dressed in my very best,
Wore the furs I never wear,
Hair done at Bloomingdales,
Even a manicure; splashed on the good perfume
Before I rode the bus up Madison
To the rear entrance of the hospital;
Traversed for miles the corridors underground
Where orderlies in green wheeled metal carts
Piled with soiled linen, bottles, pans and tubes.

Then, elevators found, I followed a colored line
To the proper nurses' station,
Embraced your wife: pale, having wept for weeks,
Worn out with your care.
She led me to your bedside. I swept in with an air,
Wrapped you in fur, censed you with my perfume.
Jaunty and thin, with the fine eyes and pursy lips
Of one of Holbein's Unknown Gentlemen,
You could not speak
Except for some unintelligible grunts
Through the hole they had made in your throat;
Impatient with your wife
Who, after years of understanding,
Could not understand.

Months of practice with my dying father
(shamed by his memory lost, he refused to speak,
Like Ezra Pound at the last) taught me to monologue:
Of our days in Roethke's room so long ago
Far off across a continent in Seattle:

One day when the bell had rung
We stood by the stairs in shabby Parrington Hall
As the hordes rushed past us to their classes.
"Oh Carolyn," you said in such a grieving tone,
"Beautiful women will never love me."
And I replied, "One day
You're going to be a famous poet,
And you'll be pursued by lovely women."
"There! Wasn't I right?" I now say,
And you look up sweetly at the lovely woman
Who stands on the other side of your bed.

Dear one, back then you were so plain!
A pudgy face, a button nose, with a little wen
Right at the tip.
But we all knew, from the moment you spoke
On the first day in class, you were our genius.
Now pain has made you beautiful.
And the black satin domino
To shade your eyes when you nap,
Pushed back on your head, looks like a mandarin's cap.
With your shapely thin grey beard
You are phenomenally like Li Po,
A poet you adored.

"Well, dear, there's no Ohio left — except in poems";
I keep up a stream of jokes and reminiscences.
You scribble notes on your yellow pad,
Nod your mandarin nod.
Grief is not permitted till it's over,
And I'm outside, stunned, standing on Fifth Avenue
In the fierce cold of January.
Here I say what I could not say upstairs in your room:
A last goodbye. And thank you for the poems
You wrote to me when we were young.

                    Now go in peace, my friend,
Even as I go
Along the soiled pavement of the Avenue
Banked in the gutters with old snow.

Born in Spokane, Washington, Carolyn Kizer was educated at Sarah Lawrence College and was a Fellow of the Chinese Government in Comparative Literature at Columbia University and subsequently lived in Nationalist China for a year.

In 1959, she founded *Poetry Northwest* and served as its editor until 1965. From 1966 to 1970, she served as the first Director of the Literature Program at the National Endowment for the Arts. She has been poet-in-residence at Columbia University, Stanford University, and Princeton University, among many others.

In 1985, Kizer received an Award from the American Academy and Institute of Arts and Letters. She also received the Pulitzer Prize for Poetry in 1985 for *Yin* (BOA Editions, 1984). Her other books include *The Ungrateful Garden* (1961), *Knock Upon Silence* (1965), *Midnight Was My Cry* (1971), *Mermaids in the Basement* (Copper Canyon Press, 1984), and *Carrying Over: Translations from Chinese, Urdu, Macedonian, Hebrew and French-African* (St. Andrews Press, forthcoming in 1986).

She makes her home in Berkeley, California, with her spouse, John Marshall Woodbridge.